GUINEA PIGS

COBAYOS

By/Por ERIN FALLIGANT

Illustrations by/Ilustraciones por SUZIE MASON

Music by/Música por MARK OBLINGER

CANTATA
LEARNING

WWW.CANTATALEARNING.COM

CANTATA LEARNING

Published by Cantata Learning
1710 Roe Crest Drive
North Mankato, MN 56003
www.cantatalearning.com

Library of Congress Cataloging-in-Publication Data
Names: Falligant, Erin, author. | Mason, Suzie, illustrator.
Title: Guinea pigs = Cobayos / by Erin Falligant ; illustrations by Suzie
    Mason ; music by Mark Oblinger.
Other titles: Cobayos
Description: North Mankato, MN : Cantata Learning, [2019] | Series: Pets! =
    Las mascotas! | Audience: Age 4-7. | Parallel text in English and
    Spanish.
Identifiers: LCCN 2017056433 (print) | LCCN 2018002227 (ebook) | ISBN
    9781684102761 (eBook) | ISBN 9781684102525 (hardcover : alk. paper)
Subjects: LCSH: Guinea pigs as pets--Juvenile literature.
Classification: LCC SF459.G9 (ebook) | LCC SF459.G9 F35 2019 (print) | DDC
    636.935/92--dc23
LC record available at https://lccn.loc.gov/2017056433

Book design and art direction, Tim Palin Creative
Editorial direction, Kellie M. Hultgren
Music direction, Elizabeth Draper
Music arranged and produced by Mark Oblinger

Printed in the United States of America.
0390

ACCESS THE MUSIC!
SCAN CODE WITH MOBILE APP
CANTATALEARNING.COM

TIPS TO SUPPORT LITERACY AT HOME

Daily reading and singing with your child are fun and easy ways to build early literacy and language development.

USING CANTATA LEARNING BOOKS AND SONGS DURING YOUR DAILY STORY TIME

1. As you sing and read, point out the different words on the page that rhyme.

2. Memorize simple rhymes such as Itsy Bitsy Spider and sing them together.

3. Use the critical thinking questions in the back of each book to guide your singing and storytelling.

4. Follow the notes and words in the included sheet music with your child while you listen to the song.

5. Access music by scanning the QR code on each Cantata book. You can also stream or download the music for free to your computer, smartphone, or mobile device.

Devoting time to daily reading shows that you are available for your child. Together, you are building language, literacy, and listening skills.

Have fun reading and singing!

CONSEJOS PARA APOYAR LA ALFABETIZACIÓN EN EL HOGAR

Leer y cantar diariamente con su hijo son maneras divertidas y fáciles de promover la alfabetización temprana y el desarrollo del lenguaje.

USO DE LIBROS Y CANCIONES DE CANTATA DURANTE SU TIEMPO DIARIO DE LECTURA DE CUENTOS

1. Mientras canta y lee, señale las diferentes palabras en la página que riman.

2. Memorice rimas simples como Itsy Bitsy Spider y cántenlas juntos.

3. Use las preguntas críticas para pensar en la parte posterior de cada libro para guiar su canto y relato del cuento.

4. Siga las notas y las palabras en la partitura de música incluida con su hijo mientras escuchan la canción.

5. Acceda la música al escanear el código QR en cada libro de Cantata. Además, puede transmitir o bajar la música gratuitamente a su computadora, teléfono inteligente o dispositivo móvil.

Dedicar tiempo a la lectura diaria muestra que usted está disponible para su hijo. Juntos, están desarrollando el lenguaje, la alfabetización y destrezas de comprensión auditiva.

¡Diviértanse leyendo y cantando!

Guinea pigs are **rodents**, like mice and squirrels. They are small, but they need a big, clean cage. They need to chew hay, or their teeth grow long. And they need one or two other guinea pigs as friends. They get lonely, just like we do! To learn more about guinea pigs, turn the page and sing along!

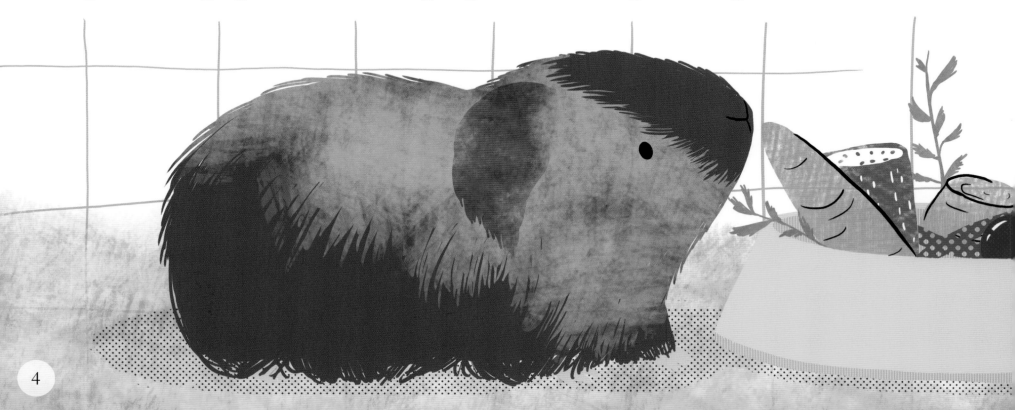

Los cobayos son **roedores**, como los ratones o ardillas. Son pequeños, pero necesitan una jaula grande y limpia. Necesitan masticar heno, o sus dientes crecen largos. Y necesitan uno o dos otros cobayos como amigos. ¡Se sienten solitarios, igual que nosotros! Para aprender más sobre los cobayos, ¡da vuelta la página y canta la canción!

We're guinea pigs! Yes, guinea pigs!
We need a place to play.
We need a quiet nest for sleep.
We love to hide away.

¡Somos cobayos! ¡Sí, cobayos!

Necesitamos un lugar para jugar.

Un nido tranquilo para dormir.

Nos encanta desaparecer.

Guinea pigs sure love to play.
We don't like to get bored.
So give us time out of our cage
to **scamper** and **explore**.

Nos encanta jugar.

No nos gusta aburrirnos.

Dame tiempo fuera de mi jaula

para **corretear** y **escurrirnos**.

We eat our **pellets**. We eat hay.

We eat green lettuce too.

Please give us fruit just now and then

and some more hay to chew!

Comemos **gránulos**. Comemos heno.
Lechuga verde también.
Danos fruta de vez en cuando,
¡y más heno para morder!

Guinea pigs sure love to play.
We don't like to get bored.
So give us time out of our cage
to scamper and explore.

12

Nos encanta jugar.

No nos gusta aburrirnos.

Dame tiempo fuera de mi jaula
para corretear y escurrirnos.

We talk with happy squeaks and grunts.

We have so much to say.

We chatter when we are upset.

Our teeth say, "Stay away!"

Hablamos con chillos y gruñidos.
Tenemos mucho que decir.
Parloteamos cuando nos molestan.
¡Nuestros dientes dicen: "¡Váyase!"

Guinea pigs sure love to play.
We don't like to get bored.
So give us time out of our cage
to scamper and explore.

Nos encanta jugar.

No nos gusta aburrirnos.

Dame tiempo fuera de mi jaula

para corretear y escurrirnos.

Please hold us close to brush our fur.
It's black and white and brown.
Go very slow. Don't brush too hard!
Then please put us back down.

Por favor cepilla nuestro pelo.

Es negro, blanco y marrón.

Hazlo despacio. ¡No cepilles fuerte!

Luego, bájame con amor.

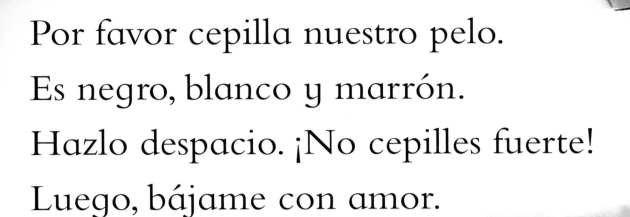

Guinea pigs sure love to play.
We don't like to get bored.
So give us time out of our cage
to scamper and explore.

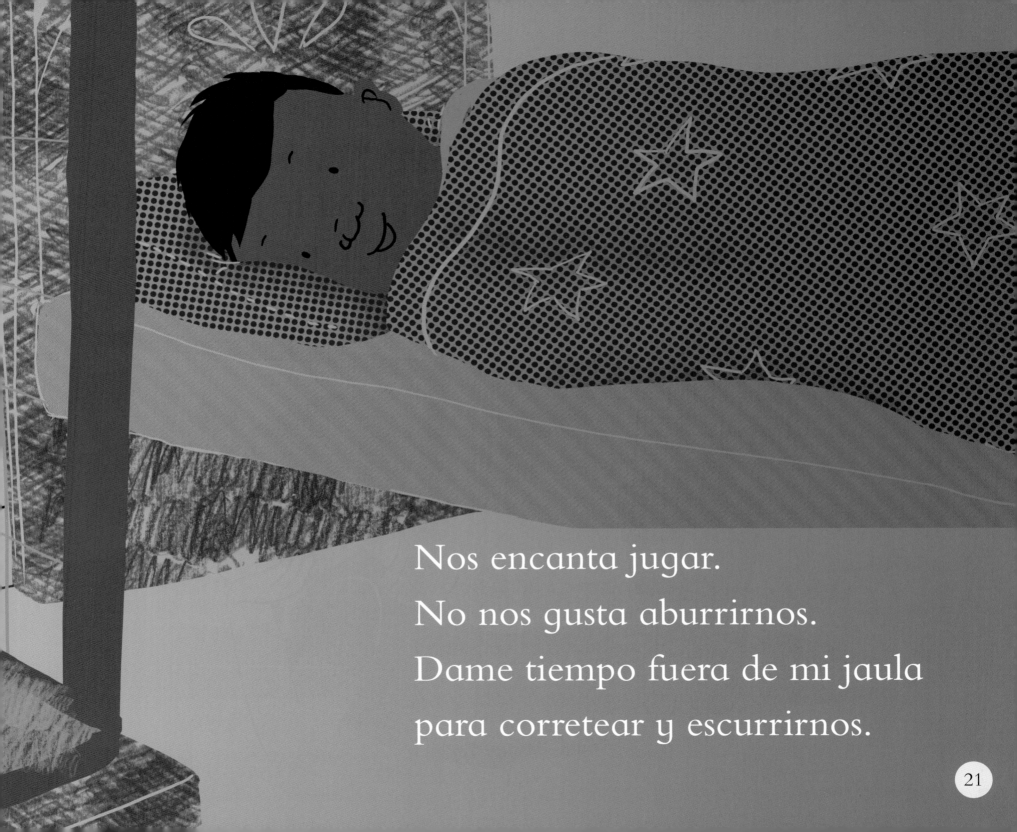

Nos encanta jugar.

No nos gusta aburrirnos.

Dame tiempo fuera de mi jaula

para corretear y escurrirnos.

SONG LYRICS
Guinea Pigs/Cobayos

We're guinea pigs! Yes, guinea pigs!
We need a place to play.
We need a quiet nest for sleep.
We love to hide away.

¡Somos cobayos! ¡Sí, cobayos!
Necesitamos un lugar para jugar.
Un nido tranquilo para dormir.
Nos encanta desaparecer.

Guinea pigs sure love to play.
We don't like to get bored.
So give us time out of our cage
to scamper and explore.

Nos encanta jugar.
No nos gusta aburrirnos.
Dame tiempo fuera de mi jaula
para corretear y escurrirnos.

We eat our pellets. We eat hay.
We eat green lettuce too.
Please give us fruit just now and then
and some more hay to chew!

Comemos gránulos. Comemos heno.
Lechuga verde también.
Danos fruta de vez en cuando,
¡y más heno para morder!

Guinea pigs sure love to play.
We don't like to get bored.
So give us time out of our cage,
to scamper and explore.

Nos encanta jugar.
No nos gusta aburrirnos.
Dame tiempo fuera de mi jaula
para corretear y escurrirnos.

We talk with happy squeaks and
    grunts.
We have so much to say.
We chatter when we are upset.
Our teeth say, "Stay away!"

Hablamos con chillos y gruñidos.
Tenemos mucho que decir.
Parloteamos cuando nos molestan.
¡Nuestros dientes dicen: "¡Váyase!"

Guinea pigs sure love to play.
We don't like to get bored.
So give us time out of our cage
to scamper and explore.

Nos encanta jugar.
No nos gusta aburrirnos.
Dame tiempo fuera de mi jaula
para corretear y escurrirnos.

Please hold us close to brush our fur.
It's black and white and brown.
Go very slow. Don't brush too hard!
Then please put us back down.

Por favor cepilla nuestro pelo.
Es negro, blanco y marrón.
Hazlo despacio. ¡No cepilles fuerte!
Luego, bájame con amor.

Guinea pigs sure love to play.
We don't like to get bored.
So give us time out of our cage
to scamper and explore.

Nos encanta jugar.
No nos gusta aburrirnos.
Dame tiempo fuera de mi jaula
para corretear y escurrirnos.

Guinea Pigs / Cobayos

Jazz
Mark Oblinger

Verse / Verso

We're guinea pigs! Yes, guinea pigs! We need a place to play. We need a quiet nest for sleep. We love to hide away. ¡Somos cobayos! ¡Sí, cobayos! Necesitamos un lugar para jugar. Un nido tranquilo para dormir. Nos encanta desaparecer.

Chorus / Estribillo

Guinea pigs sure love to play. We don't like to get bored. So give us time out of our cage to scamper and explore. Nos encanta jugar. No nos gusta aburrirnos. Dame tiempo fuera de mi jaula para corretear y escurrirnos.

Verse 2

We eat our pellets. We eat hay.
We eat green lettuce too.
Please give us fruit just now and then
and some more hay to chew!

Comemos gránulos. Comemos heno.
Lechuga verde también.
Danos fruta de vez en cuando,
¡y más heno para morder!

Chorus

Verse 3

We talk with happy squeaks and grunts.
We have so much to say.
We chatter when we are upset.
Our teeth say, "Stay away!"

Hablamos con chillos y gruñidos.
Tenemos mucho que decir.
Parloteamos cuando nos molestan.
¡Nuestros dientes dicen: "¡Váyase!"

Chorus

Verse 4

Please hold us close to brush our fur.
It's black and white and brown.
Go very slow. Don't brush too hard!
Then please put us back down.

Por favor cepilla nuestro pelo.
Es negro, blanco y marrón.
Hazlo despacio. ¡No cepilles fuerte!
Luego, bájame con amor.

Chorus

GLOSSARY/ GLOSARIO

explore—to move around a place to learn about it

escurrirse—recorrer algunos lugares para reconocerlos

pellets—small balls of food

gránulos—pequeñas bolitas de alimento

rodent—a small animal with sharp front teeth

roedor—un pequeño animal con dientes frontales filosos

scamper—to run fast and playfully

corretear—correr rápida y juguetonamente

CRITICAL THINKING QUESTION

Draw a picture of two guinea pigs. Draw the things they need in their cage. Now add speech bubbles. Imagine what they are saying when they squeak, grunt, or chatter.

PREGUNTA DE PENSAMIENTO CRÍTICO

Haz un dibujo de dos cobayos. Dibuja las cosas que necesitan en su jaula. Ahora agrega globos de diálogo. Imagina qué dicen cuando chillan, gruñen o parlotean.

TO LEARN MORE / OTROS LIBROS

Baker, Brynn. *Pet Guinea Pigs Up Close.* North Mankato, MN: Capstone, 2015.

Carr, Aaron. *El Conejillo de Indias.* New York: Av2 by Weigl, 2014.

Froeb, Lori C. *I Am Nibbles.* White Plains, NY: Studio Fun International, 2015.

Thomas, Isabel. *Gordon's Guide to Caring for Your Guinea Pigs.* Chicago, IL: Heinemann Library, 2014.